Britain
since 1930

1929	Worldwide slump begins
1930	Planet Pluto discovered
1931	Ramsay MacDonald (Labour) sets up an all-party National Government
1936	King Edward VIII abdicates to marry Mrs Simpson
1937	Edward VIIIs brother becomes King George VII
1939	Second World War starts
1940	German bombing, known as the Blitz, of London and other major cities
1944	Education Act establishes free secondary education for all children
1945	Second World War ends. Labour government elected
1947	India becomes an independent country
1948	National Health Service established
1951	Conservative government elected
1954	*Lord of the Flies* published
1956	Calder Hall, Britain's first nuclear power station, comes into operation
1959	M1, Britain's first motorway, opened
1960	TV programme *Coronation Street* first shown
1962	*Dr No*, the first James Bond film, opens
1963	The Beatles pop group sweeps to fame and fortune
1964	Labour government elected
1966	England win football's World Cup
1969	Troops sent to keep the peace in Northern Ireland
1970	Conservative government elected
1973	Britain joins the European Community. Oil crisis leads to many workers being on a 3-day week
1974	Labour government elected
1977	Silver jubilee (25th) year of Queen Elizabeth II's reign
1979	Conservative government elected under Margaret Thatcher
1982	Britain recaptures Falkland Isles after they are invaded by Argentina
1985	TV programme *Eastenders* first shown
1986	British Telecommunications becomes a private company – one of several state-owned industries to be sold off by the Conservative government
1987	Storm sweeps over southern England, causing great damage
1991	Britain fights alongside other United Nation countries in the Gulf War, forcing Iraq out of Kuwait
1994	Channel Tunnel completed

Britain since 1930

BRITAIN THROUGH THE AGES

Stewart Ross

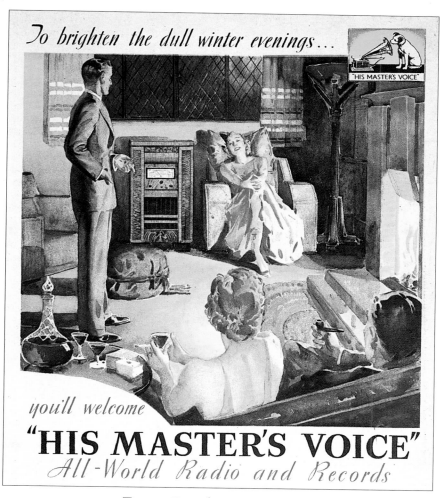

To brighten the dull winter evenings...

"HIS MASTER'S VOICE"

you'll welcome

"HIS MASTER'S VOICE"
All-World Radio and Records

Evans Brothers Limited

First published in this edition in 2003 by
Evans Brothers Limited
2A Portman Mansions
Chiltern St
London W1U 6NR

First published in hardback in 1995
© Evans Brothers Limited 1995

Published in paperback in 1995. Reprinted 1998, 2000

Printed in China

A catalogue record for this book is available from the British Library.

ISBN 0 237 52574 7

Acknowledgements
Design: Ann Samuel
Editorial: Rachel Cooke
Illustration: Nick Hawken
Production: Jenny Mulvanny

Acknowledgements

For permission to reproduce copyright material, the author and publishers gratefully acknowledge the following:

Cover (main) Corbis, (background) Robert Harding Picture Library, (top & bottom) Topham Picturepoint, (middle) Science Photo Library. Title page Topham Picturepoint. page 6 Martin Breese/Retrograph Archive Limited, (bottom) Popperfoto. page 7 Topham Picturepoint. page 8 (top) Topham Picturepoint, (bottom) Hulton Deutsch. page 9 (top left) Robert Harding Picture Library, (top right) Martin Breese/Retrograph Archive Limited, (bottom) Popperfoto. page 10 (top) Popperfoto, (bottom) Hulton Deutsch. page 11 (top) Topham Picturepoint, (bottom) Hulton Deutsch. page 12 (top) Martin Breese/Retrograph Archive Limited, (bottom) Hulton Deutsch. page 13 (top right) Topham Picturepoint, (top left) Martin Breese/Retrograph Archive Limited, (bottom) Hulton Deutsch. page 14 (top) Hulton Deutsch, (bottom) Popperfoto. page 15 Martin Breese/Retrograph Archive Limited. page 16 (top) Topham Picturepoint, (bottom) Robert Harding Picture Library. page 17 (top) Hulton Deutsch, (bottom) Robert Harding Picture Library. page 18 (top) Hulton Deutsch, (bottom) Martin Breese/Retrograph Archive Limited. page 19 (top) Robert Francis/Robert Harding Picture Library, (bottom) Topham Picturepoint. page 20 (top) Hulton Deutsch, (bottom) Jerome Yeats/Science Photo Library. page 21 (top) Yorkshire Mining Museum, (bottom) Reg Wilkins/Robert Harding Picture Library. page 22 (top) Dr Jeremy Burgess/Science Photo Library, (bottom) Ian Griffiths/Robert Harding Picture Library. page 23 (top) Popperfoto, (bottom) Martin Breese/Retrograph Archive Limited. page 24 (top) Michael Marten/Scienc e Photo Library, (bottom) Hulton Deutsch. page 25 (top) Alexander Tsiaris/Science Photo Library, (bottom) Robert Harding Picture Library. page 26 Topham Picturepoint. page 27 (top) The Bridgeman Art Library/Private Collection © The Estate of Francis Bacon, (bottom) Hulton Deutsch. page 28 (top) Press Association/Topham Picturepoint, (bottom) Topham Picturepoint. page 29 (bottom right) Associated Press/Topham Picturepoint, (left) Walter Rawlings/Robert Harding Picture Library.

Contents

Hardship and change

In the 1930s, cars like this Humber were luxuries few could afford.

The popular young king, Edward VIII, and Mrs Wallis Simpson. Edward wanted to marry the American Mrs Simpson but she had been divorced. Edward was not allowed to marry her and remain king. On 11 December 1936 he put his heart before his crown and abdicated (gave up the throne).

Changing Britain

During the reign of Queen Victoria (1837-1901), Britain was one of the wealthiest and strongest countries in the world. The British Empire stretched right round the globe. Goods from British factories were sold everywhere.

By 1930, all this was changing. The First World War (1914-18) had cost Britain millions of pounds, and hundreds of thousands of its soldiers were killed. Britain and its allies had won the war, but only with massive help from the USA. Britain still had an empire, but many parts of it, for example India, wanted to be free of British control.

Britain is run by the government, which meets in parliament. The prime minister is the head of the government. Britain is a democracy – the people choose the government they want by voting in an election. In 1930, everyone over the age of 21 could vote (women under the age of 30 had been included since 1929). There were three main groups, known as political parties (see panel), to choose from. In 1929, the people had elected a Labour government, with Ramsay MacDonald as prime minister.

Party politics

The three main political parties of the 1930s were the same as those today: Conservative, Labour and Liberal (now officially Liberal Democrat). However, the ideas of each party have changed over the past 60 years. In 1930:

■ The Conservative party did not want many changes – to conserve means to keep things as they are. It dealt with problems as they came along. After elections in 1931 and 1935, the Conservatives had the most members of parliament (MPs) and so led the National Government.

■ Labour was Britain's newest party. It was closely connected with trade unions and called for many changes (reforms). It wanted to spread wealth more evenly between the rich and poor.

■ The Liberal party had brought about many reforms in Victorian and early 20th-century Britain. They still wanted changes but they had lost ground to the Labour party. The number of Liberal MPs became steadily smaller through the 1930s.

A worldwide slump

The 1930s began with a worldwide slump. Wages fell and millions of people lost their jobs. By 1932 almost a quarter of all workers had no job. In some towns, such as Jarrow in the north of England, four workers out of every five were unemployed. People looked to government to solve the problem.

> **M**rs J's husband's been out of work 14 weeks – and there's five of them starving on 15 shillings [75p] a week …
>
> Report of a health visitor, 1936

Before long, Prime Minister MacDonald was in trouble. His government did not know how to deal with the slump. Every day more people lost their jobs. Businesses collapsed and fewer goods were traded around the world. It was a serious emergency.

The National Government

MacDonald called all parties together in a National Government, which won the elections of 1931 and 1935. The government tried to deal with the slump. It spent less and cut the dole (see below) for the unemployed. By 1937 things were improving. Even so, there were still many people without work, particularly in Scotland and the north of England.

Unemployment forced workers to try all sorts of ways to find jobs.

In 1936, men from Jarrow, Tyneside, marched to London to draw attention to their unemployment.

📖 Words, words, words....

Dole is an old word which describes money or gifts given to the poor. In 1930s, it became best known as the name people used for unemployment benefit. Millions of workers lived on the dole. It was sometimes as little as 15 shillings (75p) a week.

Life in the 1930s

Three classes

In the 1930s about 45 million people lived in Britain. Most British people thought of themselves as upper, middle or lower class. There were even three types of railway carriage – 1st class, 2nd class and 3rd class! A person's class was based on things like their education, how they spoke and where they lived. Most of all, it depended on their job and how much they earned.

About seven per cent of the population were upper class. They had enough money to live without doing a job. Most other people (68 per cent) were working class. They did manual jobs, such as labouring or working in factories, and they earned between £50 and £150 a year. They did not own their own homes. Their houses were often small and crowded, without bathrooms or electricity. As the slump began to end, the National Government tried to give people better housing (see page 18).

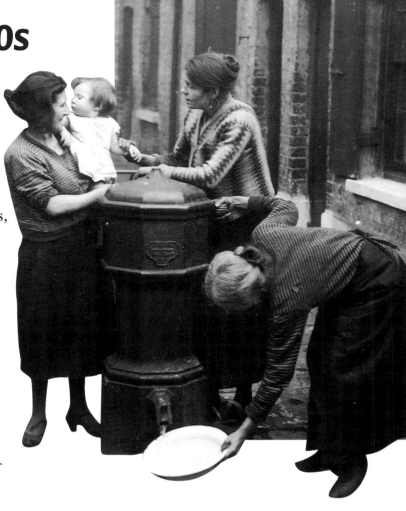

In poor areas, one water pump was the only water supply for everyone in a street.

The middle class

About a quarter of the population (25 per cent) was middle class. All sorts of people were middle class, including doctors and shop assistants. They earned between £150 and £10,000 a year and did not do manual labour. The middle class was thought of as 'respectable'. Many tried to look tidy and speak carefully.

Electrical gadgets on show at a domestic science school, 1934.

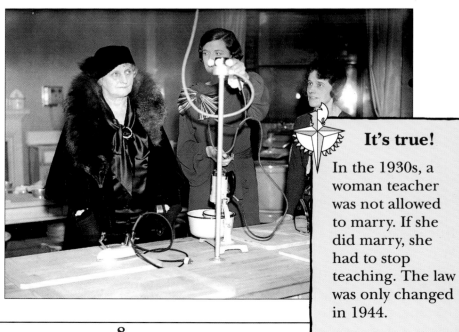

It's true!

In the 1930s, a woman teacher was not allowed to marry. If she did marry, she had to stop teaching. The law was only changed in 1944.

The middle class dreamt of owning suburban homes like one of these.

Most middle class people bought their own homes. A new semi-detached house cost about £500. More and more people could also afford to buy cars. The shops were full of new inventions for the middle class to buy: washing machines, vacuum cleaners, toasters and electric irons, to name just a few.

Do You Want A DELIGHTFUL HOME Near Town?

FREEHOLD £625 Weekly *(including rates)* 22/7 Deposit £50

With Tiled Kitchen and Bathroom, constant Hot Water, etc. Then see the splendid houses by

G. T. CROUCH, LTD., AT SUTTON COMMON MORDEN

ONLY 4 MINS. MORDEN TUBE STN.
Buses No. 155-6, 64, 70, stop at Estate. Write for details: G. T. CROUCH, Ltd., London-Worthing Road, Morden, Surrey.

The threat of war

By the late 1930s, the slump was over but Britain faced a new problem – danger from abroad. This was mainly from Germany and its Nazi leader, Adolf Hitler, who believed his country should control Europe. In 1937 Hitler took over Austria. Many people in Britain did not want war again, so soon after the horrors of the 1914-18 war. In 1938 Neville Chamberlain, the prime minister, met with Hitler to try to control the situation. They agreed Hitler could take over part of Czechoslovakia.

> I believe it is peace for our time … peace with honour.
>
> Prime Minister Chamberlain after meeting Adolf Hitler in September 1938

But Hitler's army moved into all of Czechoslovakia. War was coming closer. Finally, in September 1939, Hitler attacked Poland. Twenty-four hours later Britain and Germany were at war.

Neville Chamberlain at Croydon Airport, 1938. Here, he declared his talks with Adolf Hitler had brought 'peace for our time'.

The Second World War

Winston Churchill became Prime Minister in 1940. His stirring speeches helped lift people's spirits when defeat seemed certain.

Six years of war

The Second World War lasted from September 1939 to August 1945. Everyone was involved – ordinary people as well as the army, navy and airforce. The fighting spread all over the world.

The Nazis struck in the spring of 1940. They conquered Denmark, Norway, France, Luxembourg, Holland and Belgium. The British army was defeated and was brought home from Dunkirk. Hitler prepared to invade Britain.

Led by Prime Minister Winston Churchill, Britain stopped the German attack in the Battle of Britain (July-September 1940). Hitler turned to bombing British cities (the Blitz) and sinking ships carrying food and supplies.

*W*e shall fight on the beaches, we shall fight on the landing grounds, we shall fight in the fields and in the streets, we shall fight in the hills; we shall never surrender.

Winston Churchill to Parliament, 4 June 1940

In 1940 Italy joined Germany and they were followed by Japan in 1941, but the USA and the Soviet Union (Russia) came into the war on Britain's side. The German and Japanese advances were stopped, and in 1943 the Allies (Britain, the USA and the Soviet Union) began to push the enemy back.

The German forces surrendered on VE (Victory Europe) Day, 8 May 1945. Japan surrendered in August, after atomic bombs had destroyed the cities of Hiroshima and Nagasaki. The most costly war in Britain's history was over.

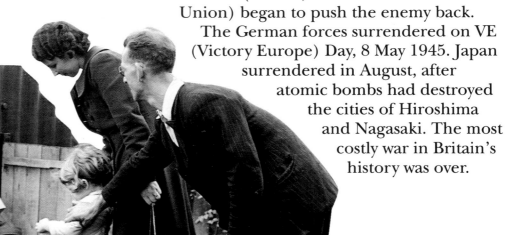

A family enters a shelter at the bottom of their garden in an air-raid practice, 1939. Swiftly-made shelters like this were far from safe if bombs fell nearby.

London on fire, 1941 (left). Once the first bombs had dropped, German bombers could aim at the fires they had started.

The morning after an air raid in London. The picture below was thought to be too upsetting to be shown in the newspapers.

Air raid!

Before the war, experts said all large British cities would be destroyed by bombing. This did not happen. Even so, London, Coventry, Birmingham, Bristol, Manchester and other cities were badly damaged. German bombs destroyed 86,000 homes and killed 60,500 people. British bombs were later to kill many more people in Germany.

At first the Germans attacked with aircraft. When the planes were spotted, air raid sirens sounded. People ran into air raid shelters. In London they hid in Underground stations. Everyone carried a gas mask in case gas bombs were dropped. Luckily, they never were.

At night the whole country was 'blacked out'. There were no street lights. People hung black curtains over the windows of shops and houses. This was to stop enemy bombers using lights to find out where they were. But once the bombs started falling, there was plenty of light from fires and explosions. Night fighter aircraft and anti-aircraft guns tried to shoot down the bombers.

Words, words, words ....

The German word *Blitzkrieg* means 'lightning war'. The British shortened it to Blitz. They used it to mean the bombing raids of September 1940 to May 1941.

In 1944, the Germans began using a new weapon – the flying bomb. It caused terrible damage. People called them doodlebugs.

Britain at war

A war-time poster encourages people to grow their own food.

11 November 1939, women farm workers hold a minute's silence in memory of the victims of World War I. During the war, women took over jobs previously done by men.

Life goes on

The war changed the British way of life. Churchill led a new government, made up of all the parties, and elections were put off until after the war. The government kept a close eye on what people said or wrote. It censored (cut out) everything that did not help the war effort. There were posters everywhere. These encouraged people to help win the war by watching out for spies and by saving food.

Enough for everyone!

Apart from the bombing, people noticed the shortages most. Before the war Britain imported a lot of food and materials from abroad. During the war, many ships were sunk, so less was imported. The materials that did get through were needed by the armed forces. Everyone else, rich or poor, had to go without.

To see that scarce goods were spread around fairly, the government brought in rationing. This gave everyone a small ration of fuel, clothes and foods, such as butter, meat, sugar, tea and jam.

Working for victory

In the 1930s many women did not have jobs. The war changed this. Because men were away fighting, women took over their work in the fields and factories. By 1943 almost all young unmarried women and many married women were working. Men not in the armed forces or other vital services joined the Local Defence Volunteers, known as the Home Guard. They were to help defend the country if it was invaded.

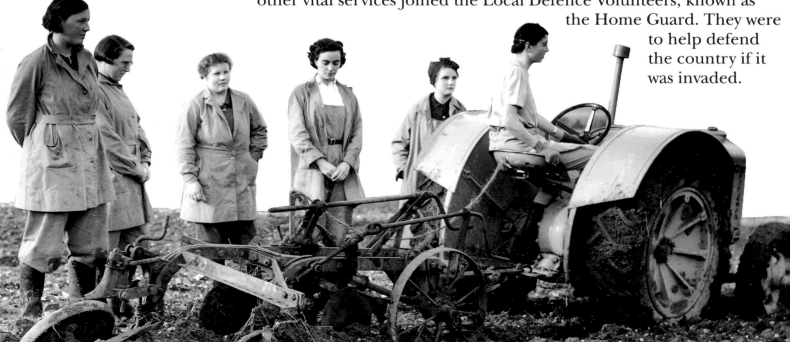

Every boy in this classroom has his gasmask in a box on his desk.

Children working on a farm in Kent shelter from an air-raid and watch the aeroplanes pass over them.

The children's war

The war was a difficult time for children. Often, their fathers were away from home fighting and out of contact for months at a time – they could have been alive or dead.

When the war began, children living in big cities were evacuated: they were moved into the countryside to get away from the bombing. During the first three days of September 1939, 1.5 million women and children were evacuated. Every child had a label tied to them in case they got lost. Many evacuees returned home after a few months.

In the cities, the bombing upset daily life. Some schools were bombed, so children had to stay at home. Many children had to spend night after night in air-raid shelters.

The war could be boring for children, too. First-class football and cricket stopped. Toy factories changed to making weapons, and rationing meant there were no sweets or even iced cakes.

No person shall put sugar on the exterior of a cake after the same has been baked.

A Ministry of Food regulation issued in 1941

It's true!

At the start of the war signposts were taken down. This was in case the Germans landed and used them to find out where to go!

'You've never had it so good!'

The first election after the war was held in July 1945. The result surprised many people. The wartime hero, Winston Churchill, was thrown out. The Labour leader, Clement Atlee, became prime minister. For the first time Labour had power to do what it wanted. It promised a fresh start for war-torn Britain.

We are facing a new era. Labour can deliver the goods.
Clement Atlee after the 1945 election

I have no easy words for the nation. I cannot say when we shall emerge into easier times.
Clement Atlee, 1947, admitting to a bleak outlook for post-war Britain

A sick child helped by a National Health Service nurse, 1955.

The Welfare State

The Labour government lasted for six years. It brought in all sorts of reforms. The most important change was setting up the National Health Service (July 1948). This meant that everyone was entitled to free health care, both in hospitals and with local doctors (general practitioners). It was part of Labour's plan for a Welfare State. They wanted to get rid of the poverty and unfairness of the 1930s. From now on the government would protect everyone against sickness and poverty, 'from the cradle to the grave'.

Another change was that the government took over (nationalised) the country's major industries, such as coal, electricity and the railways.

Coal miners proudly set up a sign saying that their mine has been nationalised. The National Coal Board was the body set up by the state to run the mines.

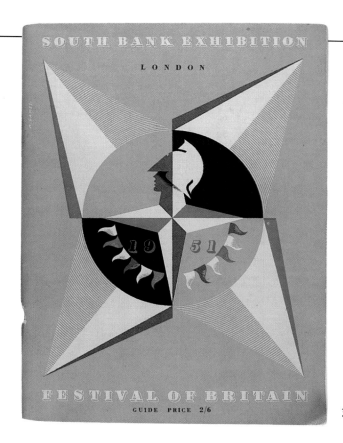

The Festival of Britain aimed to lift people's spirits after years of hardship. It was focused around the new South Bank centre in London.

Thirteen years of Tory rule

The war had cost more than Britain could afford and many of Labour's plans for a new Britain were very expensive. Some wartime rationing was still in place, too. By 1951, people wanted a change and the Conservatives (also known as Tories) won the election. Under prime ministers Churchill, Anthony Eden and Harold Macmillan they remained in power until 1964.

By and large, things went well for the Conservatives. Food rationing finally ended in July 1954. Wages increased faster than prices, so people had more to spend. Harold Macmillan was able to tell people at the 1959 general election, 'You've never had it so good!'.

No longer a world leader

After the war, Britain's place in the world was changing. Its empire disappeared as countries left it and joined the Commonwealth (see page 29). The USA and the USSR (the Soviet Union lead by Communist Russia) were now two 'superpowers', and Britain was no longer a world leader.

However, the USA, Britain and other western countries were frightened of Communism. They formed an alliance (the North Atlantic Treaty Organisation – NATO) to defend themselves against the USSR. British forces also went to Korea (1950-53) to fight the Communists there.

In 1956 British troops invaded Egypt to try to keep control of the Suez Canal. It was Britain's last attempt to act like a superpower – and a complete failure.

Words, words, words ....

Rock'n'roll was the name given to the new music that was born in the USA in the 1950s. The British youth soon adopted the music, too. American styles and fashion promoted everything exciting and modern – including a new brand of sweets!

Labour and Conservative

By 1964 many people were tired of Conservative rule. For the next 15 years the government passed backwards and forwards between Labour and Conservative (see panel on page 17).

The 1960s and 70s was a period of great change and excitement. London was the 'swinging capital' of the world. Led by the Beatles, British pop music broke new ground, and British fashions, such as the miniskirt, were followed in almost every country.

> *I*n a decade dominated by youth, London has burst into bloom. It swings; it is the scene.
>
> *Time*, the popular US magazine, 15 April 1966

London's Kings Road was the centre of 60s fashion. These girls are wearing hot pants – the latest style to compete with the miniskirt.

Problems to solve

These were troubled years, too. In Northern Ireland, there was violence between the Protestants and Catholics. Many Catholics wanted Northern Ireland to unite with the rest of Ireland, while most Protestants wanted to remain part of the United Kingdom. In 1969 British troops were sent to control the situation and have remained there ever since, but the violence continued. There were also bombings on mainland Britain.

Britain continued to grow wealthier, but not as fast as some other countries, such as the USA, Germany and Japan. In 1973, the price of oil suddenly went up. The government cut the working week to three days for a short while to cut down the use of fuel.

British troops watch over an IRA march in Northern Ireland in the late 1960s.

The government also had to deal with a succession of strikes, organised by the powerful trade unions. Abroad, striking was known as the 'British disease'. The winter of 1978-9 became known as the 'winter of discontent'. Rubbish piled up on the streets, because of a dustmen's strike, and shops had little fresh food, because of a strike by lorry drivers.

Powercuts caused by strikes in 1974 meant workers had to use duvets and candles for heat and light!

We have seen the gravediggers refusing to bury the dead … we have seen schools shut in the faces of children.

Conservative minister, Lord Hailsham, talking about the strikes of 1978-9

The new Conservatives

The 'winter of discontent' was followed with a general election in May 1979. Magaret Thatcher became Britain's first female prime minister. She was a strong leader and brought in many reforms.

The Conservatives made laws to cut the power of trade unions. They also tried to reduce the amount of money spent on the Welfare State. Some British business began to be more successful and, at times during the 1980s, it boomed. But these periods were followed by slumps and unemployment rose again.

Towards the end of the 1980s, Margaret Thatcher became increasingly unpopular. She was forced to resign as prime minister in 1990. The Conservatives chose a more moderate leader, John Major, and he won the election of 1992.

It's true!

Britain is now part of Europe in two ways! Firstly, it became part of the European Community (now called the European Union) on 1 January 1973. Secondly, the Channel Tunnel was finally opened in 1994, physically joining the British Isles to mainland Europe.

Elections and leaders, 1964-79

Margaret Thatcher

Election	Winning Party	Prime Minister
1964	Labour	Harold Wilson
1966	Labour	Harold Wilson
1970	Conservative	Edward Heath
1974, February	Labour	Harold Wilson
1974, October	Labour	Harold Wilson (replaced by James Callaghan in 1976)
1979	Conservative	Margaret Thatcher

At home

Slums to central heating

In 1930 the government started a campaign to clear away Britain's slums. The task was a huge one. Millions of homes had no bathroom or lavatory. Electric light and central heating was only for the well-off. In working class homes it was normal for children to share a bed.

The government's plans were upset by the 1930s slump and the Second World War. By the 1950s, things were improving again. Almost 12 million new houses were built between 1930 and 1979.

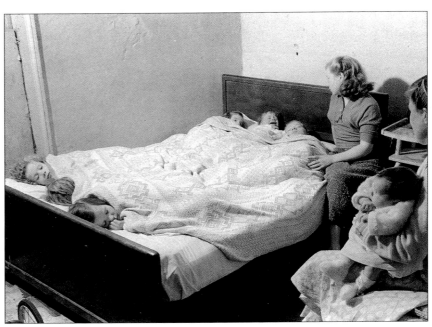

An over-crowded bed in a Liverpool slum, 1957

New towns

In 1946 some completely new towns were planned. The largest, Milton Keynes, was begun in the 1960s. New building was carefully designed, so that the countryside was not spoiled. But the tower blocks, built in the 1950s and 60s, were less successful – few people liked the way they looked and many disliked living in them.

People's homes gradually became less crowded and more comfortable. By the 1960s virtually all houses had electricity. Ten years later there was hardly a family without a television. More and more people were able to afford central heating, too. Washing machines were rare in the 1930s. By 1971, 64 per cent of homes had one, and 20 years later this figure was nearer to 100 per cent. They also had goods that had once been luxuries, such as vacuum cleaners and refrigerators.

In the 1930s, vacuum cleaners like this were considered a luxury. Today, most people would think of them as a necessity.

*W*hen I was young everything was done by coal and candles. Mum did the cooking on a coal stove. There was a grate for a fire in every room. At night I sat up in bed doing my homework by candlelight!

A woman who was at school in the 1930s

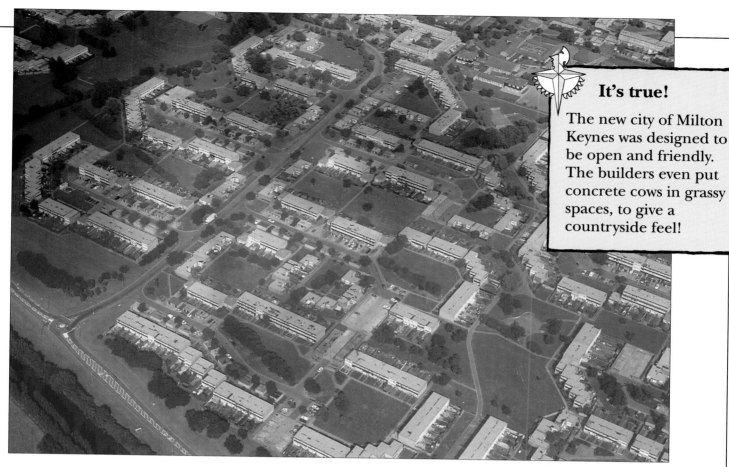

The streets of Milton Keynes are carefully planned.

By the 1960s, Mum, Dad and two children (and a dog!) was the normal – and even fashionable – British family.

Fewer children, more divorce

Between 1930 and 1990 the population of Britain rose by about 10 million. That is one reason why so many new houses were needed. A second reason was to replace slum houses. A third reason was because there were fewer people living in each house.

In the 1930s it was normal for children to live with their parents until they were married, and even after that. After the Second World War it became normal for everyone – children over 18, parents, grandparents – to want their own home.

Families became smaller, too. In the 1930s many couples had more than three children. Families with eight or more children were not unusual. By the 1990s, two children was the average. As a result, in 1975 the population of the United Kingdom fell for the first time since records began.

Married couples did not stay together so much, either. In the 1930s divorce was expensive and unusual. By the 1990s, after the divorce law had been changed, about one marriage in three was ending in separation.

At work

All change

In the 1930s Britain was a great manufacturing nation. Heavy industries like coal mining, iron and steel making, shipbuilding and engineering employed millions of workers.

In the 1990s very little heavy industry is left. People can buy or make the same things cheaper elsewhere. In Britain today, many people now work with small-scale manufacturers and the 'service' industries, such as education, health, shops, banks and insurance. New technology means that factories use more machines and fewer people. Many people use computers as part of their daily work.

Another big change is the number of women working. In the 1990s it is normal for a woman to have a job, even if she has a young family.

Painting a liner, 1951. The shipyards are now closed and their many jobs gone.

Banks of computers in a London finance firm.

Unemployment

The changes in industry, the number of people wanting work and the sort of work available lead to an increase in unemployment. There were not enough jobs to go round.

In the 1980s, southern England grew richer and more crowded. Unemployment rose in regions where the old industries had flourished – the north of England, south Wales and Scotland. In the downturn of the early 1990s, jobs were lost in southern England as well. It became clear that unemployment was going to be a long-term problem.

Words, words, words ....

A robot is a machine that can copy mechanically the actions of a person. The word came into English in 1923 from a play by the Czech, Karel Copek. Robots are now used in factories. In the 1980s, one car was advertised as being 'handmade by robots'!

Working conditions

After the Second World War life gradually improved for most workers. People were paid more and better cared for. In general, they worked shorter hours and had longer holidays. New laws made work places safer and healthier.

The trade unions played an important part in bringing this about. One of the chief weapons they held was the ability to strike for better pay and conditions. By the 1970s, many people thought striking had got out of hand and the trade unions were too powerful (see page 17). During the 1980s, the Conservative government took away some of the trade unions' power, making it harder for them to strike.

You won't get me, I'm part of the union ... till the day I die!

Chorus from *Part of the Union*, a song by the Strawbs that reached number 2 in the Hit Parade in 1973

The union banner of a miners' colliery in Yorkshire. The National Union of Mine Workers has been one of the most prominent and active trade unions in Britain.

Happy holidays

From the 1930s, people enjoyed longer and better holidays and Britain's leisure industry began to grow. In the 1950s and 60s holiday camps, such as Butlin's, became very popular. The people who worked in the camps were famous for their red coats.

Schools and colleges

All governments agreed that education was important to help people find good jobs and get more out of life. The biggest step forward was the 1944 Education Act (law). This gave every child free education to the age of 15 (raised to 16 in 1973). Government spending on education rose from £65 million in 1940 to £272 million in 1950.

In the 1980s, the Conservatives set up a National Curriculum, which laid out what subjects should be taught in schools. They also encouraged all 16-year-olds to go on to further education. By 1985 education was costing the government more than £16 billion a year.

Keeping in touch

Huge machinery helps to widen yet another road to cope with ever increasing traffic. This road is the A11 in Norfolk.

Concorde, the world's first supersonic passenger aircraft. Despite its noise and cost, the plane remains a favourite.

The age of the motor car

In 1930 there were just over a million cars on Britain's roads. By 1990 there were almost 20 million. The spread of the motor car (and lorry) changed the face of the country, particularly from 1950 onwards. Towns became clogged with traffic. Massive new motorways cut through the countryside. Shops moved from the centre to the edge of town, where there was parking space. Public transport was used less and less. Between 1930 and 1990 the railway track in use fell from 32,000 kilometres to less than 16,000 kilometres.

L et the train take the strain!

A British Rail slogan of the 1980s encouraging
passengers to travel by rail

Motor cars allowed millions of people to travel far, fast and cheaply. Cars took people to work and on holiday and to visit friends. Unfortunately, they also led to an increase in new crime, such as car theft and motoring offences. The government gradually passed laws to control driving and the use of cars. People had to wear seat belts and drivers were forbidden to drink alcohol and drive.

Travel by air

Aircraft developed rapidly, too, partly as a result of wartime research. Before 1939 air travel was a luxury for the rich. By 1980 millions of people were taking 'package holidays' to parts of the world their grandparents might never have heard of.

Concorde, the fastest passenger jet plane in the world, made its maiden (first) flight in 1969. Britain developed the jet with France and it can fly between London and New York in less than 4 hours – a standard jumbo jet takes about 7 hours. But Concorde is noisy!

Noise pollution had hardly existed in the 1930s. By 1970 cars and planes had made it a major problem.

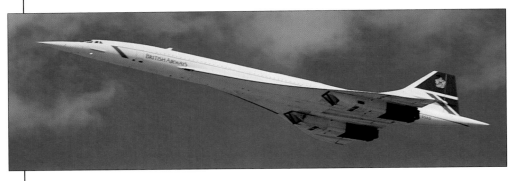

Sound and vision

It was not just people that moved quicker. Words and pictures travelled faster, too. In 1951 less than one in ten households had a telephone. Forty years later a house without a phone was rare. Faxes, car phones, answering machines and computer networks were increasingly common. Televisions spread even faster. Between 1930 and 1955 cinemas were always full, but with the arrival of television thousands had to close down.

Another important invention was the transistor in 1948. This allowed electrical goods to be made smaller and cheaper. Portable transistor radios took the place of the heavy 'wireless sets' of the 1930s. Hi-fi on disc and tape brought concert-quality music to every home. In the 1980s a new era of communication began, with CDs, personal computers and satellite broadcasts.

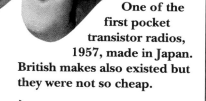

One of the first pocket transistor radios, 1957, made in Japan. British makes also existed but they were not so cheap.

Watching TV in the 1930s. Mickey Mouse, already a favourite, is on screen.

It's true!

Britain's first long stretch of motorway was the M1 between London and Birmingham. When it was opened in 1959 there was no speed limit, and many cars blew up because they were driven too fast!

Words, words, words ....

The word television was first used in 1909 but the first moving pictures were transmitted in the 1930s. Television was invented by a Scotsman, John Logie Baird. The first regular broadcasts were made by the BBC in October 1936. As television became popular, it was given a variety of names, such as tele, TV and the box.

The wonders of science?

After the Second World War science seemed to offer a better life for everyone. Scientific farming made British farms among the most efficient in the world. Nuclear power, before only used to make bombs, was used to generate electricity. The country's first nuclear power station, Calder Hall, began operating in May 1956.

Between 1960 and 1990 science and technology became an important part of everyone's lives. Breakthroughs made all over the world – and above it! – affected Britain as much as other countries. Space exploration and research has lead to other advances in science and industry.

> *That's one small step for a man, one giant leap for mankind.*
> Neil Armstrong, 20 July, 1969, as he stepped on to the surface of the moon – the first man ever to do so

By the 1980s, Britain's farmers were so efficient that they were being paid not to grow crops!

A 1950s kitchen, full of labour-saving devices

A technological revolution

Advances in technology transformed the ways people communicate (see page 23) and the world of work (see page 20). Some people call the enormous change a technological revolution.

The revolution brought many benefits. Cars were made more efficient, safe and comfortable. All sorts of new devices made life easier: microwave cookers, hair dryers, word processors and personal computers, ball-point pens, tape recorders, plastic bags and so on.

Words, words, words ....

The ball-point pen was invented by a Hungarian journalist, Ladislao Biro. The first pens – or biros – were made in Britain and went on sale in 1946 for 55 shillings (£2.75) each. At a similar price rate today, a biro would cost about £20.00!

A healthier world

Perhaps some of science's finest achievements were in medicine. By 1960 the dreadful diseases of polio and smallpox had disappeared from Britain. Antibiotics were discovered by Sir Alexander Fleming in 1928. They became widely available after the war, and deaths from infectious diseases such as pneumonia fell sharply.

Antibiotics also made surgery safer. Doctors developed many new operations, too. In 1948 surgeons performed the first operation on a living heart. Two years later the first kidney transplant took place. Heart transplants and artificial joints soon followed. But cures have still to be found for other illnesses, such as cancer and AIDS.

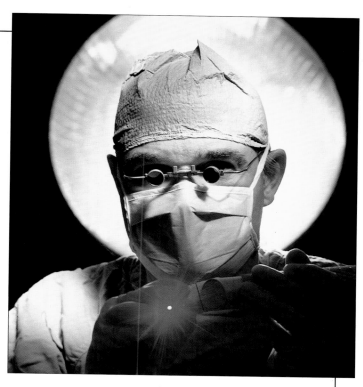

A surgeon with a laser. New drugs and techniques save lives but are very expensive.

Problems with progress

Science brought problems as well as benefits. People lived longer but as they got older many needed looking after. This was expensive and the government had to find more money than ever before to care for the elderly.

Cars, factories and scientific farming produced another problem – pollution. Nuclear power stations, too, caused pollution and could be extremely dangerous, as the accident at Chernobyl in the Ukraine (1986) showed. Caring for the environment had become a major issue. British groups such as Friends of the Earth and Greenpeace put pressure on governments to find ways of controlling the problem.

The nuclear reprocessing plant at Sellafield in Cumbria. Many people were against the plant being built.

Sport and the arts

Sport and fitness

In the 1930s football and cricket were at the height of their popularity. They attracted huge crowds and made stars of men such as Stanley Matthews (1915-). Women's sport was mostly played among the upper and middle classes, who enjoyed games such as tennis, gymnastics, hockey and swimming. Everyone enjoyed cycling and walking.

By the 1960s sport was beginning to change. The old team games lost some of their popularity. Less sport was taught in schools and the televising of matches was blamed for falling crowds. But televised sport produced new favourites, such as snooker, skiing and darts. People moved away from team games to more individual sports, like athletics and wind surfing. From the 1970s, keeping fit was seen as important for people's health. Thousands took up jogging, and fitness centres opened all over the country.

Stanley Matthews of Blackpool beats an opponent in a tackle.

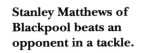

World record breaking Welsh hurdler Colin Jackson leads the field, 1993. Athletics has been one of Britain's most successful post-war sports.

It's true!

When league football started again after the Second World War, players threatened to strike unless they were paid £7.00 a week – the same as about £55.00 a week today!

The creative arts

Since the 1930s, the British creative arts (such as writing, music, acting and painting) have covered an ever-wider range of styles. In visual arts, artists such as Francis Bacon (1909-92) and David Hockney (1937-) have changed the way we look at things, as have the sculptures of Barbara Hepworth (1903-75) and Sir Henry Moore

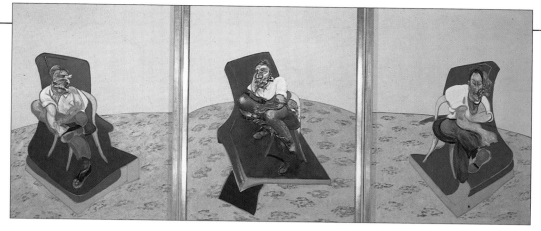

Three studies by Francis Bacon of fellow artist Lucian Freud. Although strange in some eyes, Bacon's work is eagerly collected all over the world.

(1898-1986). Designers, such as Sir Terrence Conran (1931-), who founded the Habitat chain of shops, have also influenced the visual styles but in a very different way.

A variety of tastes

Perhaps the greatest composer working in Britain since 1930 was Sir Benjamin Britten (1913-1976). Britten wrote *A Young Person's Guide to the Orchestra* and many other orchestral pieces. In contrast, many people believe John Lennon (1940-1980) and Paul McCartney (1942-), the two Beatles who wrote most of the band's music, were great composers. They brought a new sound to pop music in the 1960s.

The great classical actor Laurence Olivier, playing the lead part in *The Entertainer* (1957) by John Osborne. Osborne's *Look Back in Anger* began a new style of realistic 'kitchen sink' drama.

The Bristish novel has remained well-thought of and popular. *Animal Farm* and *1984* by George Orwell, and *Lord of the Flies* by William Golding are just three examples from a rich list.

B*ig Brother's watching you!*

George Orwell, from his novel *1984*, in which he describes a world where everyone is always being watched by the state

Television and theatre

Perhaps one of the most successful areas of creative art in Britain has been in theatre and the new medium of television. The drama productions of the Royal Shakespeare Company and National Theatre have won world-wide respect, as have the TV dramas made by the British Broadcasting Company (BBC) and others. But the British film industry has never really competed successfully with Hollywood.

Britain and the world

In 1982, Britain fought against Argentina to keep control of the Falkland Isles.

From the 1930s, Britain's place in the world was always changing. These changes were some of the most rapid and surprising in British history.

In 1930 Britain was still a world power with a massive empire. By 1950 it had become a country in decline. It was losing its empire and had been seriously weakened by the Second World War. It was like a football club that had once been at the top of the premier league, but was now being relegated every year.

By 1990 Britain was beginning to assume a new place in the world. Although no longer a world power, Britain's experience made it a respected member of the community of nations. It was now a European country, working to make the European Union and the United Nations more successful.

Immigration

When Britain returned the countries of the empire to the people who lived there, it gave them British citizenship (1948 Nationality Act). This allowed them to come and live in Britain if they wanted to.

By the 1960s quite a few immigrants were arriving in Britain, particularly from India, Pakistan and the West Indies. Their customs and cultures made Britain more varied and interesting. But immigration brought problems. Some British people were suspicious of the new arrivals. They did not understand their way of life, and sometimes there were violent clashes. As a result, the government cut back on

These West Indians at Southampton in 1962 were the last to arrive in Britain before immigration was limited by law.

immigration (1962 and later) and introduced laws to try to stop racism (acting against people because of their race) at work and in other areas.

> **T**here were the usual games in the playground ... I joined in, and I ran after a little white girl and grabbed her. She turned to me and said, 'You can't play. My mummy said I mustn't play with blackies.'
>
> Linford Christie, one of Britain's finest post-war athletes

The Commonwealth

'The British Commonwealth of Nations' officially came into being in 1931 as another name for the British Empire. As the empire wound down, it became simply the Commonwealth, with the British monarch at its head. It is a free association of independent countries and a few small territories still under British control, such as the Falkland Isles. Commonwealth leaders meet every four years to discuss common problems and interests.

Britain and Europe

After the Second World War, Winston Churchill had called for a United States of Europe. He wanted the countries of Europe to work together to balance the USSR and the USA. A European Economic Community (EEC) was set up in 1957, and Britain applied to join. It was not allowed in until 1973.

Not all British people approved of the Community. Some wanted the build up the Commonwealth (see panel), others wanted to keep strong links with the USA. A few believed that as Britain was an island, it should keep itself to itself! There were fears, too, that the EEC would take power away from the British parliament.

These worries continued, but by the 1990s many believed that Britain's future lay with Europe. History books in 100 years' time will tell us what really happened!

Words, words, words ....

As the European Economic Community grew larger and more important, its name changed to European Community, then European Union (EU). This is the name it has today.

The EU Flag

The Channel Tunnel under construction. The project is a symbol of Britain's ever-closer links with Europe.

Index

Glossary

AIDS a condition, caused by a virus, which causes the body's natural ability to fight against disease to fail

alliance an agreement to work together

antibiotics substances that can kill off some of the bacteria and viruses that cause various diseases and infections

cancer a condition caused by a growth in the body produced when certain body cells act abnormally

Catholic a member of the Christian Roman Catholic church, whose leader is the Pope

Communism the political movement which aims to achieve a classless society run by the workers and with no public ownership

democracy the system which allows all adults to choose their government

empire a collection of lands and states governed by a single powerful country

Nazi a member of the German political party founded by Adolf Hitler in 1919, which held extreme, racist views

Protestant describes the various western Christian churches that broke away from Roman Catholicism

reform a change made with the aim of improving the way a system, such as the law, works

slump financially, a period of economic collapse

state an area or country run by one government; the institutions that administer its laws

strike to stop work in order to get more pay or better working conditions

suburban describes the built-up areas around a town

trade union an organisation to help workers, usually those in the same industry

Places to visit

London
The Bethnal Green Museum of Childhood, E2
The Cabinet War Rooms, SW1
HMS Belfast, SE1
The Imperial War Museum, Lambeth, SE1
The London Toy and Model Museum, Bayswater W2
The London Transport Museum, Covent Garden, WC2
The Museum of the Moving Image, South Bank, SE1
The National Maritime Museum, Greenwich, SE10
The Science Museum, South Kensington, SW7
The Tate Gallery, Millbank, SW1
The Victoria and Albert Museum, South Kensington, SW7

Southern England
The Bath Industrial Heritage Centre
The Bristol Industrial Museum
The D-Day Museum, Portsmouth
'Hellfire Corner', a World War II command post, Dover
The White Cliff's Experience, Dover
The Maritime Museum, Southampton
The Museum of Kent Life, Sandling, Maidstone
The National Motor Museum, Beaulieu
The Royal Marines Museum, Portsmouth
The Royal Photographic Society, Bath

Central England
Coventry Cathedral
The Catalyst Museum, Widnes
The Imperial War Museum, Duxford, Cambridge
The Museum of British Road Transport, Birmingham
The Museum of Oxford, Oxford
The Museum of Science and Industry, Birmingham
The National Waterways Museum, Gloucester

Northern England
Granada Studios, Manchester
Impressions Gallery of Photography, York

Northern England (continued)
The Industrial Museum, Leeds
The Liverpool Museum
The Manchester Museum of Science and Industry
The Maritime Museum, Hull
The Merseyside Maritime Museum, Liverpool
The National Railway Museum, York
The Beatles Story, Liverpool
Western Approaches, Liverpool
The Yorkshire Mining Museum, Overton, Wakefield

Wales
The Maritime and Industrial Museum, Swansea
The Museum of Welsh Woollen Industry, Newcastle Emlyn
Rhondda Heritage Park, Trehafod, Mid Glamorgan
The Welsh Industrial and Maritime Museum, Cardiff

Scotland
Science and Technology Discovery Centre, Aberdeen
The Scotland Street School Museum of Education, Glasgow
The Scottish Mining Museum, Dalkeith
The People's Palace, Glasgow
The People's Story, Edinburgh
The Tenement House, Glasgow
Transport Museum, Glasgow

Northern Ireland
Armagh Planetarium, Armagh
Carrickfergus Gasworks, County Antrim
Causeway School Museum, Giant's Causeway, County Antrim
Coalisland Corn Mill, County Tyrone
Foyle Valley Railway Centre, Londonderry
Station 597, Crumlin, County Antrim
Ulster Folk & Transport Museum, Cultra, County Down